RITUAL & HONOUR

WARRIORS OF THE NORTH AMERICAN PLAINS

MAX CAROCCI

THE BRITISH MUSEUM PRESS

This book is published to accompany the exhibition *Warriors of the Plains: 200 years of Native North American honour and ritual* at Lotherton Hall, Leeds, from June to September 2011; Ulster American Folk Park, Omagh, from October 2011 to February 2012; Royal Albert Memorial Museum, Exeter, from September to December 2012 and Manchester Museum, Manchester, from January to April 2013.

Max Carocci has asserted the right to be identified as the author of this work.

First published in 2011 by the British Museum Press
A division of the British Museum Company Ltd
38 Russell Square, London WC1B 3QQ
britishmuseum.org

A catalogue record for this book is available from the British Library

ISBN 978-0-7141-1542-9

Designed by Price Watkins
Printed in Spain by Graphy Cems Ltd

The papers used in this book are recyclable products and the manufacturing processes are expected to conform to the environmental regulations of the country of origin.

A note on objects illustrated: all the objects featured in this book are from the collection of the British Museum. Their museum registration numbers are listed on page 95. Further information about the Museum and its collection can be found at britishmuseum.org.

Page 96: Portrait of a Hidatsa Chief (detail), photograph by John Carbutt, Missouri, 1867. Albumen print, H 7 cm, W 7.2 cm.

CONTENTS

CANADA

Rocky Mountains

Blackfoot
Plains Cree
Assiniboine

Gros Ventres
Crow
Hidatsa
Mandan
Arikara
Sioux

Cheyenne

Shoshone
Pawnee
Ponca
Iowa
Omaha
Arapaho
Oto
Kansa

Kiowa
Osage

USA

Plains

Comanche

Mississippi

Gulf of Mexico

MEXICO

Map of North America showing the vast region
occupied by Plains Indians for thousands of years.
The area stretches from the Mississippi river to
the Rocky mountains and from the Canadian plains
to the Gulf of Mexico.

INTRODUCTION

NATIVE NORTH AMERICANS who today inhabit the Great Plains have been warriors for centuries. Traditionally, warfare, dance and ceremony cannot be separated because together they represent the values that maintain group identity. Although they are separate nations with individual customs and separate languages, the peoples that live in this vast region are collectively known as Plains Indians. They once shared a common nomadic life, based on bison hunting and occasionally agriculture. Today they share a history and many of the values developed during their past as warriors.

This book illustrates the rich cultural heritage of Plains Indian warriors through objects from the British Museum collection, which cover a time span of more than two hundred years. While most of the objects featured here, such as weapons, pipes and headdresses, were either directly linked to battles or used in war ceremonies, some of the newer items clearly reflect changes not only in form, but also in the content associated with war and its related rituals. Objects once used in ceremonies to honour warriors returning victorious from battle and war raids, for example, have become today's dancing regalia used in competitions called powwow. Here, these items are shown alongside art pieces, which encourage us to reflect on the significant role warrior traditions play in constructing contemporary Native North American Plains Indian identities. Although many warrior traditions have died out, some have been revived and today are enjoying a popular comeback. In 2010 the British

Powwow dancer at a competition
Photograph by Milton Paddlety, Kiowa, Oklahoma, 1994.
H 3.6 cm, W 2.5 cm

Museum acquired the replica Kiowa Black Leggings warrior society uniform belonging to Commander Gus Palmer (1919–2006), who initiated the revival of warrior societies of his tribe in 1957 after a long period of inactivity (see page 91). The British Museum's Plains Indian collections also include very old pieces such as a rare specimen of a calumet-style pipe given to the explorers Lewis and Clark in the early nineteenth century (see page 17), and also tomahawks, shields and horse gear used in parades when the wars against colonists ceased after the last bouts of resistance in the 1890s.

Contemporary Native North Americans stress the intimate relationship that they see between combat and spirituality. This connection still retains its cultural significance for many of the men and women who choose to be drafted to the military forces of both Canada and United States. Fighting is an expression of a code of honour, based on the moral and spiritual principles that guide a person's life in accordance with values of respect, strength and reciprocity. For many modern Plains Indian soldiers, leading an honourable life is as important as it was for ancient warriors – for whom the extreme sacrifice, death, was considered the most respected and highly valued act a man could carry out. The significance of objects for contemporary people is not only that they transmit these values to the new generations, but also that they have the unique function of maintaining links with history and tradition. Each of the nations that occupy the Great Plains retains a direct connection with their ancestors by keeping alive the fighting spirit, which once granted honour to successful warriors and the tribe alike. All the objects featured in this book connect past, present and future generations because they are associated with stories, myths and traditions, which are as important for modern Native North

WARRIORS OF THE PLAINS

A selection of pipes from George Catlin's
North American Indian Collection, **1852**
Oil on cardboard, H 44.3 cm, W 57.8 cm

American artist George Catlin left an impressive
record of the Plains Indian tribes that he
encountered during his extensive travels across
North America. In his *Book of Pipes* (pictured
here), he recorded the various types of pipes used
by different groups in the early nineteenth century.

Americans as they were for the peoples they originated from. Beliefs related to war and invisible forces that animate the universe emerged from these stories and gave meaning to the objects used in both warfare rituals and battles. The objects contained spiritual powers, which were bestowed upon warriors by sacred beings in dreams and visions, and were believed to be imbued with forces that enhanced fighting power.

Images of Plains Indians, which have circulated around the world, are familiar to many. However, the overall picture of Plains cultures presented here goes against some of the more deeply-rooted stereotypes engendered by these representations. The British Museum always seeks to question received knowledge about indigenous peoples, through a commitment to consultation and intellectual cooperation with groups around the world. This book has benefited from the input of several cultural experts from Native North American communities, which greatly enhanced our understanding of the objects presented here. Ideas about war and warfare cannot be understood unless we appreciate the deep religious, social and cultural significance that Plains Indians attribute to objects used in combat. All the objects included in this book play an active role in the production and maintenance of culture, and an awareness of this legacy will restore confidence and pride in the future generations of Native North Americans.

The seen to the unseen, the dead to the living,
a fragment of anything to its entirety.

Omaha song

1

RITUAL OBJECTS

PLAINS INDIAN WARRIORS generally belonged to societies, which, much like military regiments, had their own distinctive badges and insignia. Each warrior society had musicians who sang and played at meetings and ceremonies. Rattles and drums were often made as part of a ritual kit. The kit also included sashes, belts and bonnets, which were used only for special occasions.

Ritual objects, including bonnets and sacred bundles, as well as shields, had to be kept outside. This was because they were powerful items and could be touched and seen only by certain people within the society. They were stored in rawhide cases called *parfleche* and hung on tripods outside the tepee.

Detail of a *parfleche*
See page 25

Rattle with Thunderbird
Cheyenne, late 1800s. Hide, animal tail and feathers, L 23 cm (excluding feather and tail)

In North America rattles have been used for thousands of years by warriors to accompany their ritual and ceremonial life, as well as for medicinal practice. Rattles were stored in medicine bundles, which belonged to individual societies. This rare rattle displays a motif that is associated with thunder and lightning's power to strike an enemy (see above right). This motif, also used in today's dances and ceremonies (as seen in the photograph of Kevin Haywahe, page 40), is a stylized image of lightning, which was believed to come out of thunder beings' eyes.

Drum with Thunderbird OPPOSITE
Cree (?), late 1800s. Skin stretched on a wooden hoop-like frame, D 28 cm

Plains Indians often decorated their objects with mythical Thunderbirds. The most common depiction of the Thunderbird is an hourglass-shaped motif that can be found on pipe stems and quill decorations. This drum was probably used in medicine ceremonies that were carried out by ritual specialists.

Pawnee leader Pi'-ta-ne-sha-a-du during a diplomatic visit to Washington holding a pipe

Photograph by James E. Mc Clees Studio, 1857–8.
H 16.3 cm, W 12.2 cm

The famous Pawnee leader Pi'-ta-ne-sha-a-du (Man and Chief) sits holding a pipe in a studio photograph made during an official trip to Washington DC. Plains Indian leaders on diplomatic visits always carried a pipe. Pipes were both personal and symbolic objects. They signified authority and honour. A man carrying a pipe was considered truthful and reliable. These were the qualities entrusted upon chiefs.

Pipe stem with mythical *piasa* (underwater panther)

Santee Sioux (?), *c*.1840. Wood and porcupine quill,
L 96 cm, W 2.1 cm

This pipe stem (front and back) is decorated with intricate plaits made from dyed porcupine quills. Most of the geometric motifs are decorative, but two figures in particular are highly significant. These are the Thunderbird and the *piasa* (mythical underwater panther) visible on opposite sides of the stem. Known to several Plains tribes, these two beings were respectively associated with sky and the underworld. The Thunderbird and *piasa* symbolized the struggle between opposites. A man using such a pipe ritually mediated between these forces as a reminder of man's role in keeping nature in balance.

PI'- TA - NE - SHA - A - DU
(Man and Chief.)
Principal Chief of the Pawnees.

Published by the Trustees of the Blackmore Museum Salisbury 1865.

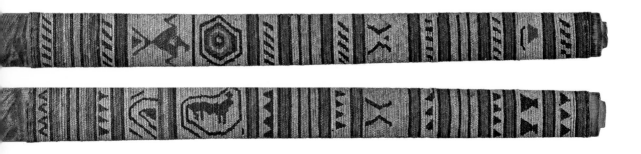

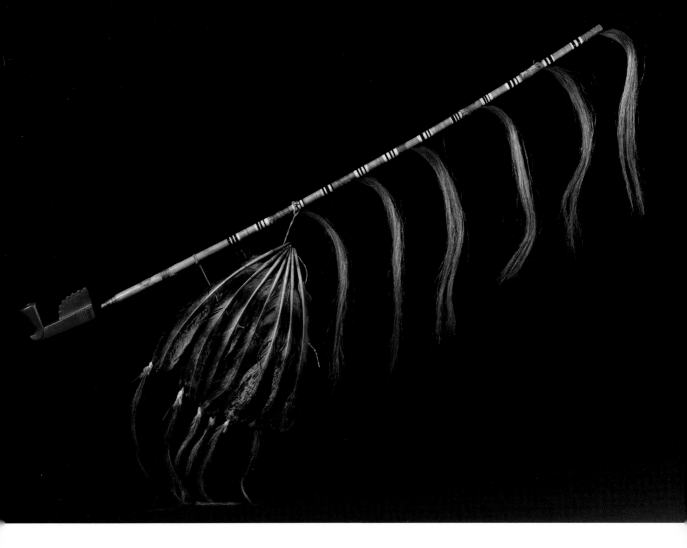

Pipe stem with feather fan and pipe bowl
Northern Plains, c.1825. Red stone, catlinite and feathers,
L 113 cm, H 7 cm

Among the Plains peoples pipes have always been an essential
part of both political and ceremonial life. Modern Plains Indians
still regard pipes as powerful spiritual objects and continue
to hold pipe ceremonies. Traditionally, warrior leaders sealed
alliances and pacts under the oath of the pipe. Before battle,
raid leaders were chosen to be 'pipe carriers' (see also detail
of robe with battle scenes on page 65). They were responsible
for guarding the pipe, which was believed to be sacred and to
give protection from enemies and guarantee success in battle.
During ceremonies and rituals, warriors smoked pipes of sacred
tobacco to establish a connection and communicate with
supernatural and invisible forces.

Buffalo bowl

Pawnee, *c.*1860. Metal and catlinite, L 25.4 cm

The buffalo has a central place in Plains Indian beliefs. Praised for its strength, it is often depicted as a mythical ancestor that supports life and gives sustenance. It is frequently represented on ritual objects, such as this pipe bowl, and parts of its skin were used in ceremonial dances and ritual celebrations.

Buffalo mask
Photograph, late 1800s. H 24.1 cm, W 19.3 cm

The use of buffalo masks in ritual dances has ancient origins. Early images of buffalo dancers can be seen on eighteenth-century painted robes from the eastern Plains, and have also been depicted in paintings by artists, such as Karl Bodmer and George Catlin. Among tribes such as the Blackfoot, women used buffalo headdresses in seasonal rituals that ensured successful hunts.

Pipe bags OPPOSITE
Early–mid-1800s. Skin, beads, hide and quills,
c. L 100 cm, W 18 cm

Although they had a ceremonial function,
men frequently owned pipes, which were
carried in bags. They contained tobacco
blended with dried herbs and shredded bark
called *Kinnikinnick*. This was a popular mix
used across the Plains. Tobacco is native
to the Americas. It was planted only by
a few tribes, such as the Crow, who traded
it with other nomadic tribes. Tobacco is one
of the most sacred plants used by Native
Americans.

**Studio portrait of Two Bear, Head Chief
of the Yanktonal Sioux holding a pipe bag**
Photograph by William Blackmore, 1800s.
H 10.2 cm, W 6.2 cm

Dakota Brave.

Dakota man
Carte-de-visite photograph, mid-1800s.
H 8.7 cm, W 5.7 cm

This Dakota man is holding deer-hoof (dewclaw) rattles, which were often used in ceremonies performed by warrior societies. Deer-hoof rattles originated with the Eastern tribes and reached the Plains with tribes migrating westward. These rattles were highly important ritual items that embodied the power of thunder.

Deer hoof harness or bandolier
OPPOSITE
Sioux, 1800s. Leather and deer hoof,
D 50 cm

Distinct harnesses, bandoliers and baldrics were included in warrior society regalia. Deer dewclaws were particularly important because they were associated with thunder beings whose help was sought by warriors. Today, such objects continue to be worn by Plains Indian dancers much in the same way as they were used in the past.

Parfleche OPPOSITE
Blackfoot (Kainai), late 1800s. Buckskin, L 70cm, D 15 cm

A *parfleche* is a type of container used to store objects or food. The word is French and originally described shields made of rawhide. *Parfleches* such as this one were used to store ritual items that were too 'powerful' to keep indoors. Ceremonial objects, headdresses and other implements used in society dances were often put in *parfleches* and hung on tripods outside tepees to keep them out of reach.

Parfleche
Lipan (Apache), 1800s. Leather, L 92 cm, W 26 cm

It's me – I am a war eagle! The wind is strong but I am an eagle! I am not ashamed, no – I am not. The twisting eagle's quill is on my head. I see my enemy below me. I am an eagle, a war eagle!

Iowa war song

2

ANIMAL PROTECTION

WARRIORS sought protection from animals and supernatural beings, such as the mythical Thunderbird. Many societies were named after their own animal protector, or from parts of animals, for instance the Kit Foxes, Doves, Mad Dogs, Bulls, Mosquitoes and One Horn Society. Some warrior societies kept sacred bundles made up of animal parts or entire skins, feathers, hooves and claws. Sacred wrappings were taken on raids to ensure success in war. Warriors also tied personal charms to their shields, weapons, war shirts or hair. These gave the warriors swiftness in combat, invisibility or acute sight.

Assiniboine men
Photograph by Geraldine Moodie, 1800s. Albumen print, H 22.5 cm, W 17.4 cm

Assiniboine men wearing weasel-skin belts and protective items. Weasels were sought after for their skins, which were traded as luxury items among many tribes.

Shirt made of scalp and ermine

Crow, late 1890s (?). Wool, skin, human hair and ermine tissue,
L 73 cm (collar to base), W 159 cm (cuff to cuff)

The combination of scalps and ermine skins on a war
shirt may be attributed to the wearer's dreams. Warriors
were often instructed through dreams to make objects
that would help them in battle, such as in the photograph
of Assiniboine warriors wearing weasel skins around their
belts on page 28.

Split-horn headdress OPPOSITE
Blackfoot, 1800s. Hide, cloth, fur, feathers,
brass studs and glass beads, L 64 cm, W 20 cm

This headdress belonged to the Brave Dog society
of the Blackfoot. Dozens of precious ermine tails
were used to decorate it. Usually only the central
strip of the animal's back was used, including the
black-tipped tail, but this headdress also includes
tufts from the animal's fur. The split horns are
probably made from buffalo horn, split to make
the headdress lighter to wear. These are also
decorated with ribbons and white glass beads.

**Piegan Indian warrior wearing the emblem
of the Brave Dogs, an ermine tail headdress**
Photograph by Frederick Seele, c.1895. Colour postcard,
H 14 cm, W 9 cm

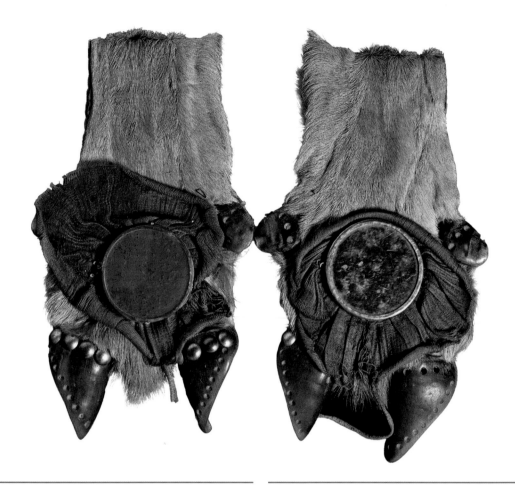

Protective charm, arm band
Blackfoot (Kainai), 1800s. Silk, glass, deer hoof, cotton and brass,
L 21 cm, W 12 cm

Round shield OPPOSITE
Sioux (?), early 1800s. Rawhide and buckskin, D 57 cm, L 110 cm (tassle)

Warriors wore round shields in combat, but not always as a
defensive weapon. These objects had a spiritual meaning, which
was conveyed through the powerful symbols and designs painted
on them. Shields were usually worn on the back and identified the
owner through unique motifs, often received in visions or dreams.
Round shields originally developed from large, man-sized rawhide
shields, which were carried by two men on foot.

WARRIORS OF THE PLAINS

Pawnee Sun Chief (La-roo-chuck-a-la-shar) OPPOSITE
Photograph by William Henry Jackson, 1868. Albumen print,
H 19 cm, W 13.7 cm

Bear-claw necklace with metal star
Blackfoot (?), 1800s. Metal, glass and claw, L 29 cm, W 26 cm

Bear claws had a deep spiritual significance for Plains Indians due
to the strength and power associated with the animal. The star,
which decorates this necklace, also appears on ceremonial robes
among the Blackfoot, Pawnee and other Plains tribes. It represents
the morning star, an important theme in Plains Indian beliefs. The
star motif can also be seen as a decoration on holy men's robes,
such as in the hide worn by the Pawnee spiritual leader opposite.

No matter how many will die, let them die!

Mandan Black Mouth society song

3

TRADITION & CONTINUITY

BY THE LATE 1800s, most Plains Indians had been forced into reservations and warfare between groups was suppressed. Warrior dances and traditions were adapted to a new lifestyle. Although they were no longer used to prepare for and celebrate battle, they still maintained a deep cultural significance. Today, men and women in each society create new garments and regalia for festivals and dance competitions called powwow. In these, performers wear feather bustles, as well as ornaments in their hair and around their waist, ankles and arms – all modern forms of the old warrior styles and Native American traditions.

Returning the gaze (detail)
Assiniboine dancer Kevin Haywahe with face paint by Jeff Thomas (Iroquois), 1991. H 86 cm, W 60 cm

In this portrait by Iroquois artist Jeff Thomas, *Returning the gaze*, the Assiniboine professional dancer, Kevin Haywahe is portrayed with highly meaningful face paint. The 'bird's eye' motif shown was associated with war and the power of the hawk to strike its prey. This photograph shows how contemporary dancers use design motifs that have cultural connotations and denote strong relationships with the past.

Kiowa women belonging to the Black Leggings Warrior Society, performing a scalp dance in honour of returning war veterans
Photograph by Milton Paddlety, Kiowa, Oklahoma, 1996. H 3.6 cm, W 2.5 cm

Feather headdress OPPOSITE
Blackfoot, 1800s. Eagle feather, hair, glass, fur, cotton and brass, H 46 cm, D 23 cm

This type of headdress originated among the Blackfoot and was later adopted by tribes of the Rocky Mountains, such as the Nez Perce. Warrior headdresses were worn by women during scalp dances, held in honour of the men's return from war raids.

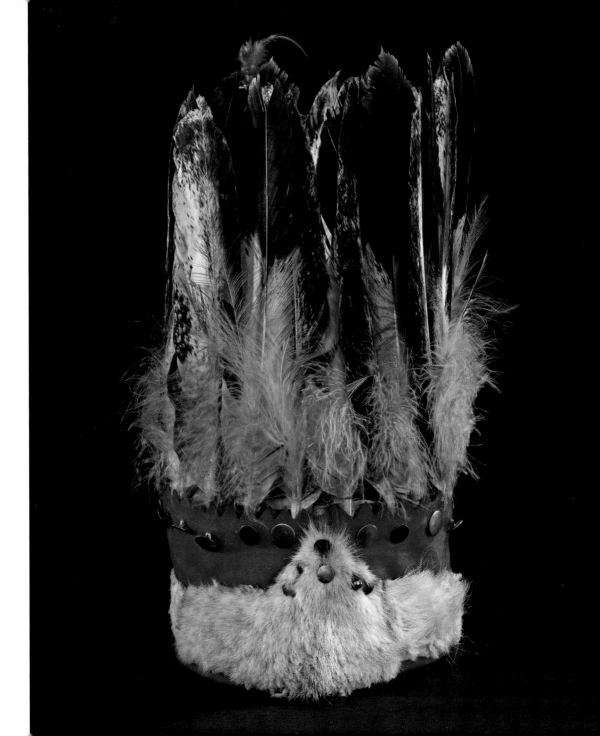

Hair ornament

Sioux, 1800s. Skin, rattlesnake rattle, metal, horse hair, feather and abalone shell, L 12 cm

Dakota-speaking peoples call this ornament *Wapegnaka*. It is worn at the back of the head and holds different kinds of upright pointing feathers in place. This example is particularly rich as it also includes a rattlesnake's rattle tied to an abalone shell disc just below the feathers (see detail opposite). The use of feathers, shells and rattlesnake may have ritual significance. They symbolically represent air, water and earth beings. This combination is a very old motif and is also found in shell engravings of pre-colonial times.

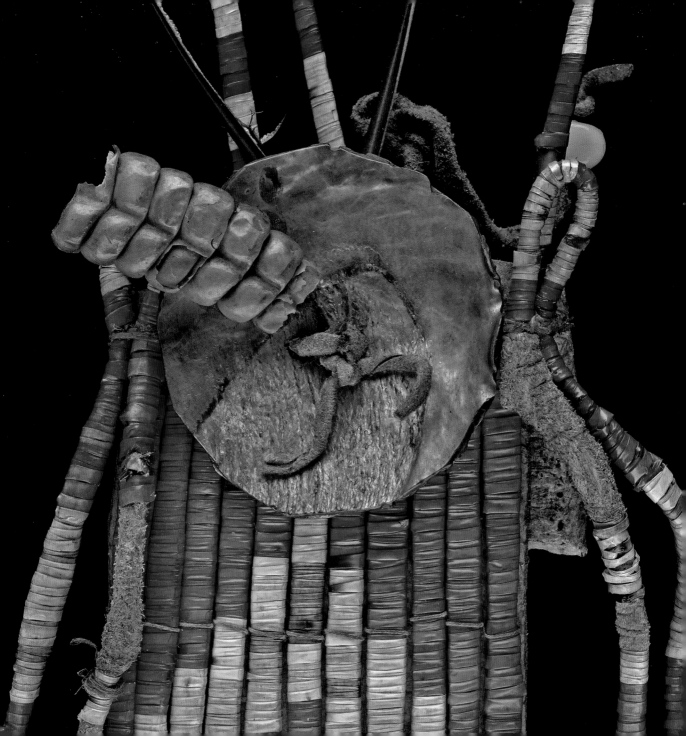

Feather bustle OPPOSITE
Blackfoot (Kainai), late 1800s. Tin, pottery,
porcupine quill, feathers and brass, D 56 cm

Feather bustles developed from warrior dances
performed among the Omaha tribe. They were
originally worn tied behind the back and often
included a trail decorated with feathers and
pendants. Over time, the waist bustle became
bigger and more elaborate, although smaller
versions worn on the arms also became
popular. Today, dancers use feather ornaments
as part of their regalia. Current versions use
commercially coloured feathers and include
mirrors, or even compact discs to fix the
feathers to the round background.

Cree dancer
Photograph by G.E. Fleming. Silver gelatin print,
1879–1902. H 25.4 cm, W 20.3 cm

Dance regalia made from feathers are very
ancient. Pre-colonial figurines display similarly
shaped bustles, which illustrate the importance
of the shape that symbolizes the sun's rays.

Harness with mirrors and feathers

Blackfoot (Kainai), late 1800s. Metal, glass, fur, feathers and buckskin, L 116 cm, W 60 cm

Many warrior societies used this type of garment as a distinctive badge, although there were several variations. Harnesses were usually made of otter-skin and in some tribes this object was specifically associated with war rituals. Over time, the otter-skin harness developed into two simple strips attached at one end, as worn by the Dakota leader opposite. These strips could be decorated with feathers, mirrors and other pendants, such as beaded strips or shell buttons. Eventually, this garment became the basic pattern for today's powwow beaded harnesses, as seen in the regalia on page 51, which are worn by dancers who perform in a style of dance called 'Fancy Dance'.

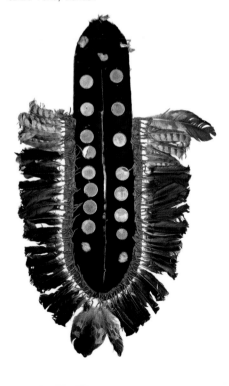

**Dakota Sioux leader Wambdihowaste
(Pretty Voice Eagle),**
Photograph by Gould, 1913. H 16.7 cm, W 12 cm

In this photograph the Dakota leader
Wambdihowaste is wearing fur strips
decorated with mirrors.

Powwow dance regalia by Dennis Zotigh
Kiowa, 2000–9. Twenty-eight pieces of regalia,
including feathered roach, beaded bandoliers,
gaiters, headband and belt, tabard and apron,
feathered back and arm bustles and goatskin
boots, H 210 cm, W 120 cm

Contemporary dancers in powwow
competitions wear items derived from
warrior dance gear developed in the
nineteenth century. Constantly adapting
to new fashions and trends, modern
dance outfits include commercially
available ribbons, mirrors and other
industrial materials in addition to
feathers, deer hair and porcupine quills.

Dance quirt

Blackfoot (Kainai), late 1800s. Wood, skin, glass, fur, feather and brass,
L 105 cm, W 50 cm

This elaborate whip, or quirt, was almost certainly used in
warrior society dances to invite people to take part in social
events. It shows a carving of men and horses and is decorated
with eagle feathers and animal fur, which functions as a handle.
Warriors used smaller versions of these whips in battle to drive
on their horses or to touch their enemies as an act of bravery.

Running Wolf, a Kainai chief, and a group of Blackfoot men
ABOVE Postcard, early 1900s. H 14 cm, W 9 cm

The One Horn society of the Blackfoot survived after their nomadic lifestyle came to an end. Their dances continued well into the early twentieth century.

Society dance belt BELOW
Blackfoot, late 1800s. Skin, fur and feather, L 97cm, W 23 cm

Belts such as this one, which is probably made from bear fur, were emblems of warrior societies such as the Bear Braves, or the Pigeon society of the Blackfoot. Each society had its own insignia made from parts of animals to which societies were often dedicated.

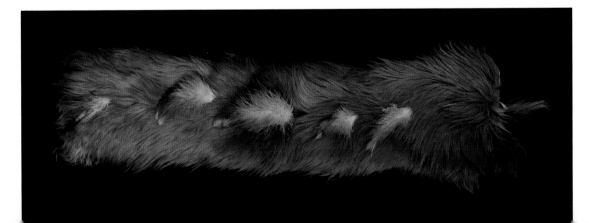

You Foxes, I want to die, thus I say!

Crow Fox society song

4

HONOUR & STATUS

EN WERE ENCOURAGED to become warriors from an early age. Among several tribes, warrior societies were age graded and young men earned the right to move into the next society by displaying courage in battle and taking great risks. To prove their honour, warriors had to steal horses and weapons, touch an enemy, kill them or take scalps. With military success came wealth and status, measured in horses and tallies of deeds performed during raids. Only the most honoured warriors could wear feather headdresses and war shirts, often decorated with scalps taken in battle.

Pair of moccasins
Crow, 1800s. Skin and beads,
L 25 cm, W 9.5 cm, H 8.6 cm

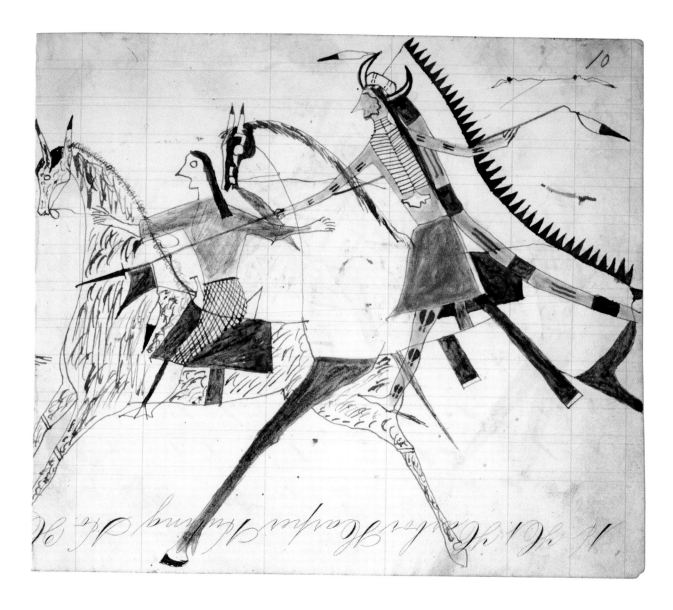

Mounted warrior wearing trailing headdress
OPPOSITE
Tall Bear, Sioux (Oglala Lakota), 1874.
Drawing on paper, H 17.5 cm, W 21 cm

Long trail headdress with fur trim RIGHT
Blackfoot (Kainai), 1800s. Hide, silver braid, cloth,
brass, golden eagle feathers, ermine fur and horse
hair, L 140 cm, W 43 cm

This headdress from the Kainai tribe, part
of the Blackfoot confederation, is associated
with the chief called Little Ears. This type
of headdress belonged to the Horn society,
one of the most powerful warrior societies.
Trailing headdresses were used by prominent
warriors and could be decorated with split
horns as can be seen in the image opposite
drawn by a Sioux warrior in the late
nineteeth century.

Robe with battle scenes FOLLOWING PAGES
Blackfoot, 1800s. Buffalo skin, L 220 cm, W 75 cm

Bison robes worn around the body advertised
a man's bravery through scenes depicting
his battle deeds. Here one can see the
warrior engaged in activities such as touching
a woman, holding scalps and hand-to-hand
combat. Horse stealing, touching enemies
and scalp taking were the most common
scenes depicted on these garments, which
were slowly replaced with commercial blankets.

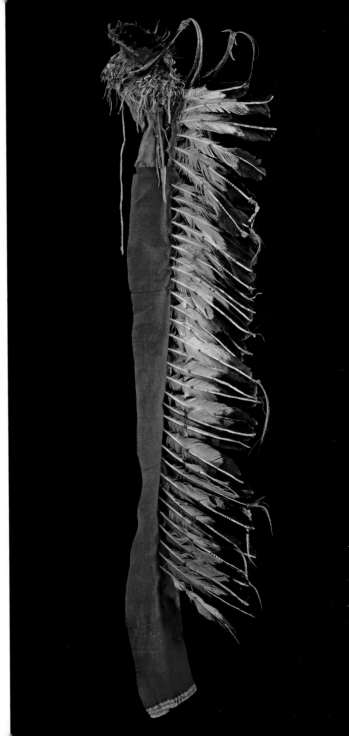

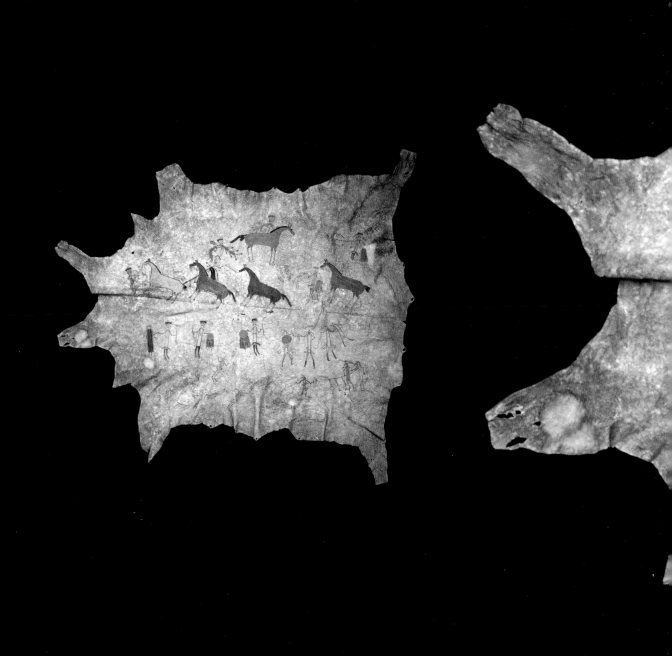

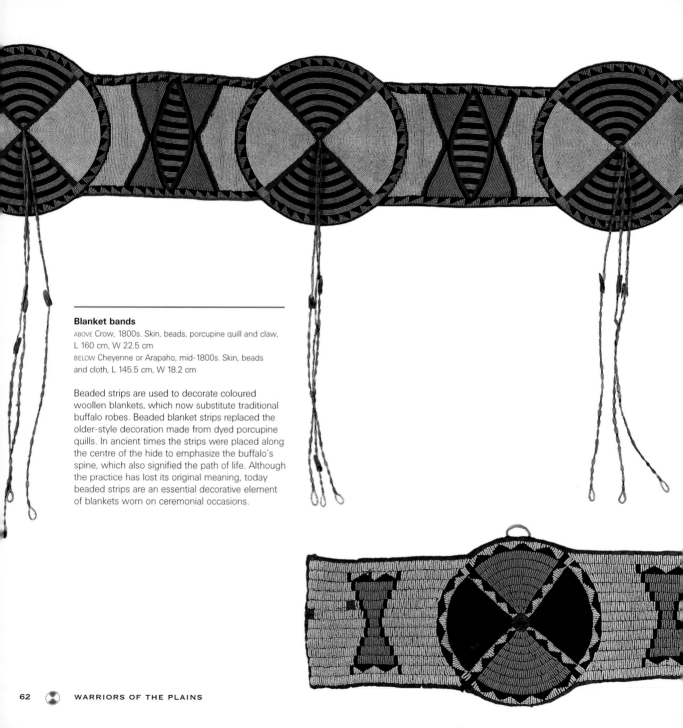

Blanket bands

ABOVE Crow, 1800s. Skin, beads, porcupine quill and claw,
L 160 cm, W 22.5 cm
BELOW Cheyenne or Arapaho, mid-1800s. Skin, beads
and cloth, L 145.5 cm, W 18.2 cm

Beaded strips are used to decorate coloured
woollen blankets, which now substitute traditional
buffalo robes. Beaded blanket strips replaced the
older-style decoration made from dyed porcupine
quills. In ancient times the strips were placed along
the centre of the hide to emphasize the buffalo's
spine, which also signified the path of life. Although
the practice has lost its original meaning, today
beaded strips are an essential decorative element
of blankets worn on ceremonial occasions.

Cheyenne leader Tak-kee-o-mah (Litte Robe)
Photograph by Gurney Studio, 1871. H 14.4 cm, W 9.7 cm

Here the Cheyenne leader, Tak-kee-o-mah is wearing a
commercial blanket decorated with a traditional beaded
strip. Blankets were commonly worn by Plains Indian
warriors, either around the shoulders or the waist.

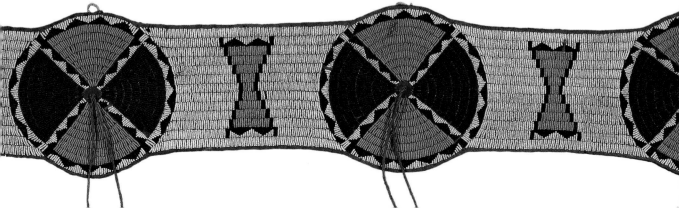

Shirt with human scalp locks
Sioux (Dakota), mid-1800s. Porcupine quill, leather, horse hair, human hair, glass and fur, H 150 cm

Ceremonial shirts were often decorated with scalps taken in battle. They indicated a warrior's bravery and gave the shirt additional power associated with hair. The red colour of this shirt is associated with life force. The arrow motifs and stripes, which have been drawn on the body of the shirt, represent the owner's brave military actions.

Detail of robe with battle scenes OPPOSITE
See pages 60–1

Men holding scalps are commonly depicted on warrior's robes, as in this detail from the robe painted by a Blackfoot warrior.

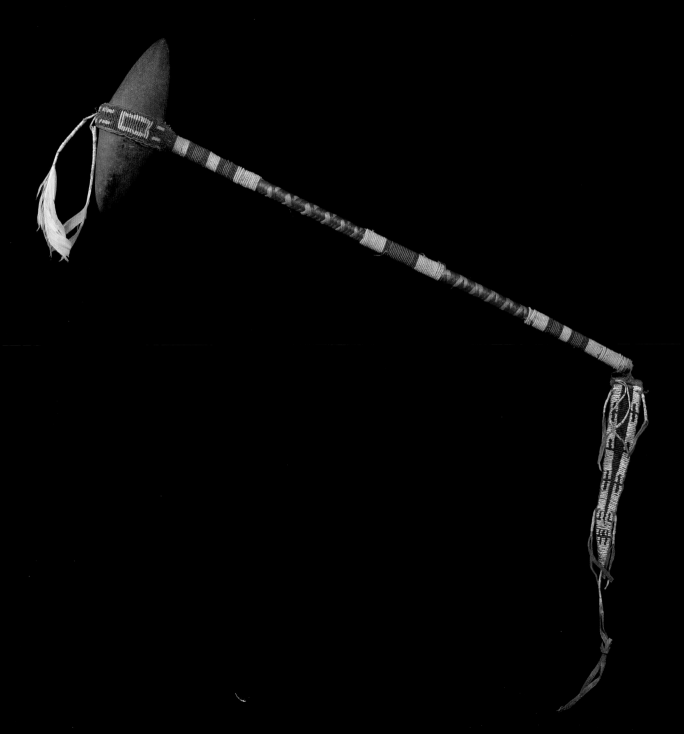

Club OPPOSITE

Blackfoot or Sioux (?), 1870–1900. Quartzite, wood, glass, buckskin (?), horse hair, feathers, porcupine quills, L 66 cm, W 21 cm

Stone-headed clubs were used as offending weapons. Here, the old-style technique of horse hair plaiting is visible. Before glass beads became widely available the most common materials used by Plains peoples were dyed horse hair and porcupine quills. These materials were also used as embellishment on shirts and leggings.

Coup stick or dance club

Blackfoot (Kainai), 1800s. Cloth, wood, beads, buckskin and hair, L 110 cm

Plains warriors always carried a club in their battle kit. These varied in length and shape according to their use. Flail-like stone clubs were common among many tribes. Warriors decorated them as prized items that represented their martial strength. Scalp locks, beaded patterns and colourful pigments were believed to augment the striking power of the club at the same time as enhancing the owner's presence.

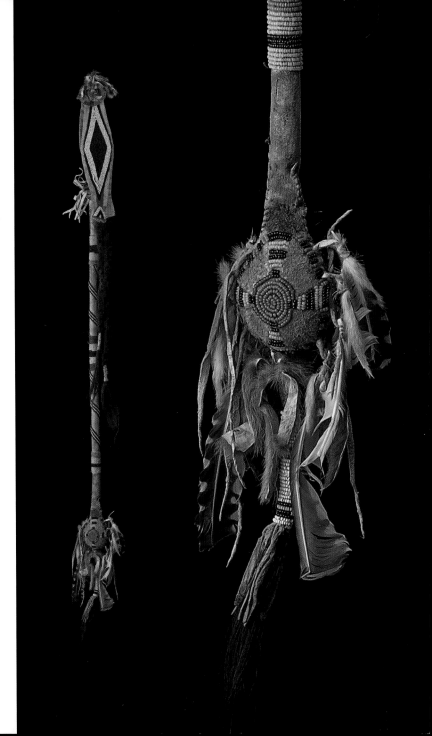

A. GARDNER, Photographer,   *Roman Rose*   511 Seventh Street, Washington.

Roman Nose, Cheyenne leader meeting US officials
Photograph by Alexander Gardner, mid-1900s.
H 23 cm, W 17.7 cm

War chiefs, such as Roman Nose, were selected by tribes to interact with government representatives.

Tomahawk pipe OPPOSITE
Blackfoot (Kainai), 1800s. Iron, wood, brass, bearskin and buckskin, L 93 cm, W 37 cm

Tomahawks are a type of axe traditionally associated with military chiefs and therefore with leadership and political authority. Archaeological finds indicate that among American Indians, high-ranking people had long been buried with large quantities of stone or copper blades. When Europeans realized the importance of these objects among North American Indians they began to produce and sell metal axe-heads to them. It was possibly the British who were the first to combine axe-heads with traditional pipes to create pipe-tomahawks. This was a significant innovation for Plains Indians. Because pipes were used to seal alliances, pipe-tomahawks represented both peace and war. They were a reminder of the delicate and changing nature of diplomatic relationships.

Knife-sheaths OPPOSITE

1800s. Various materials including skin, porcupine quills, brass, feathers and glass beads. *c.* L 30 cm, W 10 cm

Warriors carried knives for hunting and war as well as for domestic purposes. Knife-sheaths were heavily decorated in a mix of styles. Geometric and floral motifs are typical of northern Plains tribes such as the Cree and Blackfoot. The Sioux knife-sheath on the left is decorated with red quills, which can be associated with blood streaming from the nose of a bull buffalo. This detail may be significant to the owner. Often such tufts and fringes are simple decorative devices. Bead colour, embroidery technique and case shape may indicate tribal provenance.

Moccasins

1800s. Various materials including wool, skin, buffalo sinew, glass, cotton porcupine quills. *c.* L 25 cm, W 10 cm

Moccasins were a crucial item in the warrior kit. When warriors intended to set off on the warpath, women produced large quantities of spare moccasins for their long periods of absence from the village. The expression 'women are making moccasins' indicated that a war raid was imminent. The shape of the moccasin's sole was unique to each tribe and pursuers could indentify the provenence of warriors from their footprints.

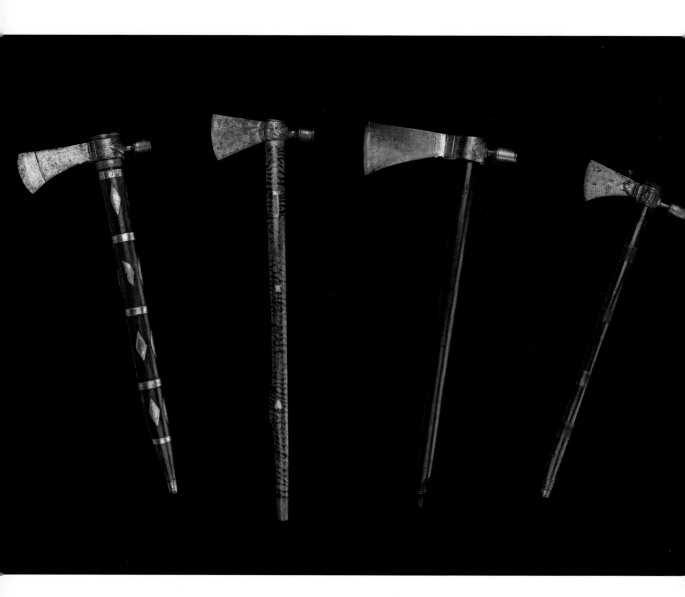

Tomahawk pipes OPPOSITE
1800s. Iron, brass and wood, c. L 55 cm, W 8 cm

Tomahawks and axes were essential items for Plains Indian warriors. There were several types of tomahawk: halberd, spontoon, spiked, hatchet-type, with hammer polls and pipe tomahawks such as these ones. Tribes which traded with the English or French had access to different sorts of axe blades and it is often possible to tell a tomahawk's tribal provenance from blade shape and manufacture stamps. This is because large quantities of the same tomahawk heads were sold only among certain tribes.

Ledger drawing with a warrior on horseback attacking an American soldier
Good Bear, Sioux (Oglala Lakota), 1874.
Drawing on paper, H 13.8 cm, W 21.5 cm

Ledger drawings produced by Plains Indians in the nineteenth century depict scenes of battle and village life. They are realistic renditions of past Native American lifestyles and often use pre-existing printed patterns from ledgers to convenient ends. In this drawing the artist has made use of the printed hatchet from the ledger to show the warrior attacking an American soldier.

It's goose bumps and chills when you watch women celebrate what we did in battle. There is no other feeling, no other home coming that would make you feel the way these women celebrate a successful return from battle.

Sergeant Major Lenny Asepermy, Comanche veteran, 2010

5

FROM
WARRIOR
TO
SOLDIER

WHEN EUROPEANS began to sell guns to Plains Indians, hand-to-hand combat became rare, although fighting continued on horseback and warriors continued to carry shields and charms for their spiritual power. Today, even though technology has changed ways of fighting and warriors no longer carry shields in battle, they still wear charms for spiritual protection. As US and Canadian citizens, Native North Americans have served in all the major world conflicts since the First World War. Ritual remains important for these soldiers. For instance they continue to hold traditional ceremonies before and after fighting. Veterans returning from the battlefield display their tribal and American or Canadian symbols equally, representing continuity in a long and established warrior tradition.

Detail of parade saddle
See page 83

Dance shield with feathers ABOVE AND OPPOSITE
Blackfoot (Kainai), late 1800s. Skin, feather and cotton, D 90 cm

Muslin-covered shields, such as this one, began to replace hide
shields as early as the mid-1800s and became increasingly
popular. They were mostly used in dances, during which warriors
retold their battle deeds in front of their comrades. The back of
this shield (opposite) is decorated with images that the owner
may have dreamed and that were designed to protect him.

The Horn Society of Alberta Indians.

Group of Blackfoot men, members of the Horn Society ABOVE
Postcard, 1907. H 9 cm, W 14 cm

During the early reservation period, warrior societies became a tourist attraction in parts of North America. Postcards such as this one were sold as local 'folklore' in Canada.

Dance spear BELOW
Blackfoot (Kainai), 1800s. Wood, iron, horse hair, feathers and beaver skin. L 128 cm, W 4 cm

Short spears wrapped with fur were used in society dances, never in battle. Staffs and many other items, including particular spears, were associated with specific societies and were carried by warriors as badges of honour.

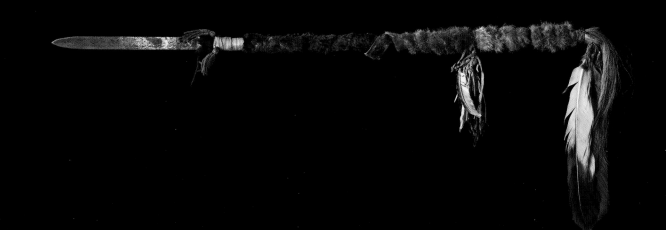

Rifle case

Crow (?), 1800s. Hide and glass beads, L 115 cm (not including fringe)

Guns were imported to North America by Europeans. Plains tribes, such as the Crow and Blackfoot, decorated their rifle cases with extensive beadwork, fringes and painted patterns. Bead colour and size are often associated with particular tribes who used specific palettes in their decorations of clothing and other items. The Crow are renowned for their use of pastel colours and unique beading techniques.

Warrior stealing a horse
Tall Bear, Sioux (Oglala Lakota), 1874.
Drawing on paper, H 17.5 cm, W 21 cm

In the past, horse stealing was considered a brave act that deserved public recognition. In the ledger, a man is shown capturing a horse. Horses were revered as powerful beings with the speed of thunder. Plains Indian peoples still consider them to be man's most prized possession.

Parade saddle OPPOSITE
Blackfoot or Cree, late 1800s–early 1900s (?). Wool, skin, metal and glass, L 47 cm, H 27 cm, X 28 cm

Padded and extensively beaded saddles, such as this one, would not have been used by warriors on the battlefield. The lavish beaded decoration on this parade saddle shows Plains peoples' respect and devotion to their animals, as well as the social status and wealth of the owner.

Military cap OPPOSITE
Sioux, early–mid-1900s. Glass beads and cotton,
D 20 cm, X 10 cm

This US military cap marks a significant link
between old warriors and modern soldiers. It has
been fully beaded with American flags as well
as powerful traditional Native American symbols.
These are directly linked to cosmic protection, such
as the cross that points to the north, south, east
and west. Native Americans have never doubted
their allegiance to their land, here symbolized by
the American flag.

**Kiowa soldiers march alongside US military
officials during veteran celebrations in Oklahoma.**
Photograph by Ian Taylor, 2009

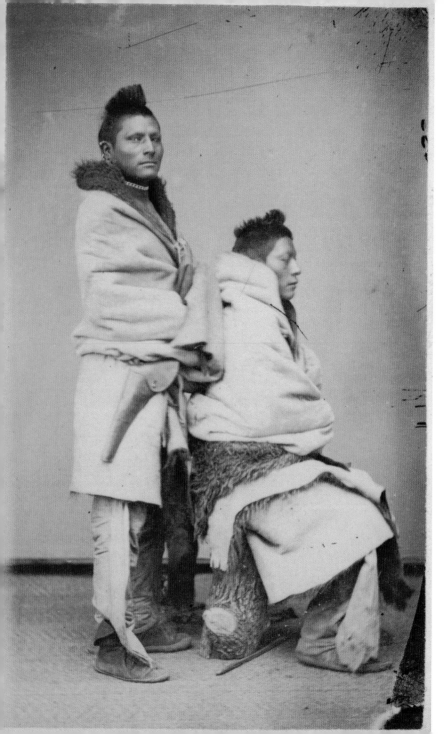

Two Pawnee scouts for the US army
Photograph by Jackson Brothers 1800s.
Carte-de-visite, H 10.1 cm, W 6.1 cm

These two Pawnee men were employed
by the US army as scouts. American
and Canadian armies benefited from
ancient rivalries between Native nations
and played them against each other.
Alliances frequently shifted, but tribal
enemies' varying degrees of collaboration
with the army played an important role in
determining the fate of war campaigns.

Gun holster OPPOSITE
Don Tenoso, Sioux, 2006. Metal, leather,
glass and feather, L 26 cm, W 9 cm

This beaded replica holster captures
the intimate relationship between Native
Americans and warfare. A warrior is
shown holding a medicine bundle with
his horses and his enemies are depicted
in the portraits of a blonde General Custer
and his soldiers, who were defeated at
the battle of Little Bighorn in 1876. The
images have been found through writing
in ledger art and on Plains Indian clothing.
Holsters were not often fully beaded, but
the artist here plays on the continuity
between old ways and a self-reflective
present.

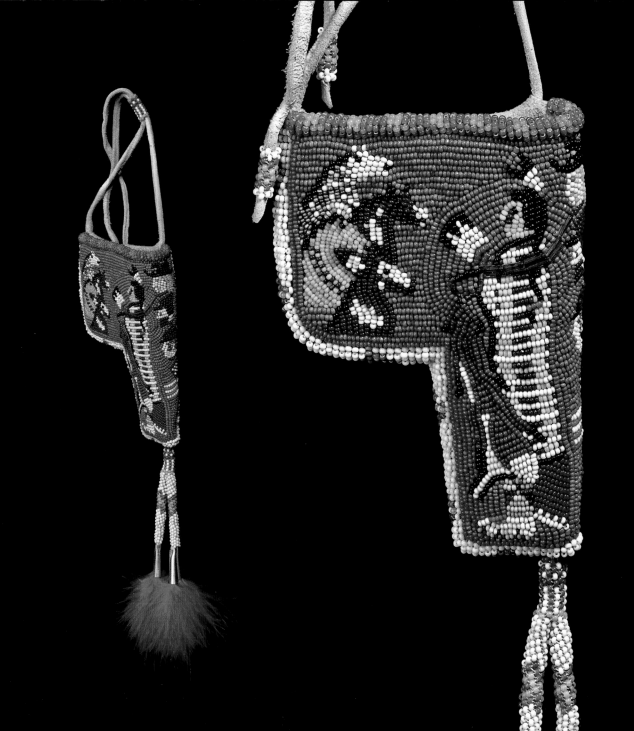

Purification kit by Christopher Scott Gomora (Ojibwa), Ken Harper (Cherokee) and Jack Flores (Yakima/Cherokee)
Ritual fan: turkey and goose feathers, leather, horse hair, glass beads, deer skin and bone, L 115 cm, W 18 cm.
Abalone shell: L 18 cm, W 16 cm, X 6 cm
Herb bundles: wild sage (*Artemisia tridentata*) bound with yellow thread, L 14.5 cm, W 4 cm
Braided sweetgrass (*Hierocloe odorata*), L 40 cm, W 2 cm
Twisted tobacco: L 17 cm, W 6 cm
String with cotton bundles containing tobacco and angelica root: L 360 cm

Today soldiers continue to practise old-style rituals before going to war. Many contemporary Native American soldiers enrolled in the military purify themselves with the smoke of burning sage, sweetgrass and cedar, which is wafted around the body with feather fans. It is believed that this practice will ensure safe return home. This kind of purification ritual has roots in ancient beliefs. Colourful bundles of tobacco wrapped in cotton signify prayers. They are strung together and left as offerings to the spirits of the ancestors.

Replica of Black Leggings warrior society regalia belonging to Gus Palmer Senior OPPOSITE
Kiowa, 2009. Lance, breech cloth and beaded sash by Vanessa and Carl Jenkins, Kiowa; red cape and shawl by Lara Klinekole Palmer, Apache/Comanche; breastplate by Allen, Kiowa and Karen Yeahquo, Cheyenne/Arapho; belt, moccasins and cuffs by Winona Kodaseet, Kiowa; backdrop dagger by Alice Tendooah Palmer, Kiowa; war headdress made by anonymous relative, Kiowa.
Staff L 250 cm, Regalia H 200 cm, W 90 cm

This outfit is a faithful reproduction of contemporary Black Leggings warrior society regalia worn by Kiowa men during their dances. It includes a feather headdress, a cape, a breastplate and the black leggings that give the society its name. Today, revived societies of warriors gather war veterans who fought to protect their tribe and land. As in the past, their achievements are acknowledged through celebrations and dances around the emblems of their victory, such as feather headdresses, military insignia and flags. Tribal communities today, like in the past, honour their veterans in recognition of their bravery and courage.

Military insignia and feather headdresses sit side by side in the ceremonial grounds during the 2009 veteran celebrations of the Kiowa tribe in Oklahoma.
Photograph by Milton Paddlety, Kiowa, October 1996

Drawing of a warrior on horseback
Tall Bear, Sioux (Oglala Lakota), 1874. Drawing on paper, H 17.5 cm, W 21 cm

Plains Indian men traditionally used a realistic style to express ideas and facts. Women adopted more abstract and geometric styles, which they applied to the arts they produced, such as beadwork, skin paintings and quillwork. In recent years these boundaries have started to blur and both men and women can now work with each other's techniques and styles.

Ledger drawing

Linda Haukaas, Sioux (Sicangu Lakota), 2009. Drawing on paper,
H 29 cm, W 45 cm

Although warfare has changed since the last century, Plains Indian
women continue to celebrate the return of soldiers in the same
way as their grandmothers did at the warriors' comeback. In this
piece Lakota artist Linda Haukaas appropriates the customary
masculine realistic style representing a traditional victory dance
performed by women in honour of returning warriors.

FURTHER READING

Berlo, Janet C. and Phillips, Ruth, *Native North American Art* (Oxford: Oxford University Press, 1998)

Carocci, Max, *Warriors of the Plains: the Arts of Plains Indian Warfare* (London: British Museum Press, forthcoming 2012)

Hansen, Emma I., *Memory and Vision: Arts, Cultures, and Lives of Plains Indian People* (Seattle: Washington University Press, 2007)

Horse Capture, Joseph D. and Horse Capture, George P., *Beauty, Honor, and Tradition: the Legacy of Plains Indian Shirts* (Washington and Minneapolis: National Museum of the American Indian and the Minneapolis Institute of Arts, 2001)

Horse Capture, George P., Vitart, Anne, Waldberg, Michael, and West, Richard, Jr., *Robes of Splendor: Native North American Painted Buffalo Hides* (New York: The New Press, 1993)

Kessel, William B. and Wooster, Robert (eds), *Encyclopedia of Native American Wars and Warfare* (New York: Checkmark Books, 2005)

Keyser, James D., *The Art of the Warrior* (Salt Lake City: University of Utah Press, 2004)

King, Jonathan C.H., *First Peoples, First Contacts* (London: British Museum Press, 1999)

Mails, Thomas E., *Dog Soldiers, Bear Men and Buffalo Women* (New York: Prentice Hall, 1973)

Rosoff, Nancy B., *Tipi: Heritage of the Great Plains* (Seattle: University of Washington Press, 2011)

Taylor, Colin F., *Native American Weapons* (Norman: University of Oklahoma Press, 2001)

ACKNOWLEDGEMENTS

Sincere thanks go to the Native American commentators who offered knowledge and time to enrich with their expertise our understanding of the cultural material published here: Lyndreth Palmer, Dixon Palmer, Dennis Zotigh, Allan Pard, Milton Paddlety and Stephanie Pratt. Grateful acknowledgement for their invaluable support goes to people at the British Museum: Jonathan King, Colin McEwan, Robert Storrie, Devorah Romanek, Harry Persaud, Ian Taylor, John Davy, Helen Wolfe and Morwenna Chaffe.

IMAGE CREDITS

Except where otherwise stated, photographs are © The Trustees of the British Museum, courtesy of the Department of Photography and Imaging (with special thanks to Mike Row). British Museum registration numbers are listed below: names of donors are given in brackets.

p 7: Am,Paddlety,F.N.1790, p 42: Am,Paddlety.f.n.2225 and p 90: Am,Paddlety,F.N.2330 (Milton Paddlety); p 8: Am2006,Ptg.25; p 12 (detail) and p 25: Am1954,05.951 and p 84: Am1954,05.941 (Wellcome Institute for the History of Medicine); p 14 (both): Am1930,-.61; p 15: Am1949,22.145; p 16 (above): Am.a37.11; p 16 (below): Am1949,22.155; p 17: Am5200.a and p 23: Am,+.4645 (Sir Augustus Wollaston Franks); p 18: Am,Dc.86.a; p 19: Am,a13.8; p 20: L–R: Am1948,17.3, Am1944,02.215 (Irene Marguerite Beasley), Am1935,0710.3.b (Miss Dollman), Am1930,-.37; p 21: Am,A9.75; p 22: Am,B35.33; p 24: Am1903,-.106; p 28: Am,B42.8 (Geraldine Moodie); p 30–1: Am1944,02.201, p 37: Am1944,02.257, p 44–5: Am1944,02.247 and p 62 (above): Am1944,02.225 (Irene Marguerite Beasley); p 32: Am1887, 1208.6; p 33: Am,B41.20; p 34: Am1903,-.56.a-b; p 35: Am2003,19.7 (Purchased with the support of the Heritage Lottery Fund, J.P. Morgan Chase, British Museum Friends and The Art Fund); p 36: Am,A37.16; p 40 and back cover: Am,Lge.1; p 43: Am1887,1208.7; p 46: Am1903,-.98; p 47: Am,B47.3; p 48: Am1903,-.94; p 49: Am,A13.22; p 50–1: Am2010,2028.1; p 52: Am1903,-.102; p 53 (above): Am,B41.17; p 53 (below): Am1903,-.95; p 56: Am1930,-.18a-b; p 58: Am2006,Drg.15; p 59: Am.7478 and p 60–1 and 65 (detail): Am.917 (Henry Christy); p 62 (below): Am1937,0617.2; p 63: Am,A12.5; p 64: Am9063 (John Davidson); p 66: Am1902,Loan01.50 (On loan from the Royal Collection); p 67: Am1903,-.81; p 68: Am,A40.15; p 69: Am1903,-.82; p 70 (L–R): Am1948,17.8; Am1887,1208.14; Am1903,-.83; Am1949,06.26 (Lt-Col W.T. Pares and Maj J. Pares); p 71 (above L–R)): Am1953,09.6.a-b (S.S. Benjamin), Am1887,1208.5.a-b, Am1887,1208.5.a (Mrs G.S. Guy); p 71 (below L–R): Am1985,11.3.a-b (Mrs M.S. Kendall), Am1981,Q.1939.a-b, Am1981,Q.1940.a-b; p 72 (L–R): Am,Dc.75; Am,Dc.74a-b; Am,Dc.72.a; Am,Dc.69.a; p 73: Am2006,Drg.19; p 78–9: Am1903,-.93; p 80 (above): Am,B41.16; p 80 (below): Am1903,-.92; p 81: Am1981,Q.1934; p 85: Ian Taylor; p 86: Am,A9.126; p 87: Am2006,04.1; p 88: L–R: Am2002,12.3.a-b; Am2002,12.3.d-f; Am2002,12.4 (Kenneth Harper, Christopher Scott Gomora and Jack Flores); p 91: 2009,2038.1.a-r and p 93: Am,2010,2005.1 (Purchased with the support of the Sosland family); p 96 Am,A38.43